Iris

"There is only one thing in the world worse than being talked about, and that is not being talked about."

Oscar Wilde

Little Books of Ireland

Irish Writers

Book and Jacket Design by Brian Murphy

© Picture Press.ie Ltd 2012

Published by Real Ireland Design
Picture House
16/17 Bullford Business Park,
Kilcoole, County Wicklow.
www.realireland.ie
info@realireland.ie

A CIP catalogue record for this book is available from the
British Library.

ISBN 0946887-357

Irish Writers

Samuel Beckett
1906-1989

Jonathan Swift
1667-1745

G. B. Shaw
1856-1950

Brendan Behan
1923-1964

Oscar Wilde
1854-1900

J. M. Synge
1871-1909

James Joyce
1882-1941

Sean O'Casey
1880-1964

W.B. Yeats
1865-1939

When I play my fiddle in Dooney,
Folk dance like a wave of the sea...

WB Yeats

The artist, like the God of creation,
remains within or behind or beyond
or above his handiwork,
invisible, refined out of existence,
indifferent, paring his fingernails.

James Joyce
A portrait of the artist as a young man

James Joyce

1882-1941

"A hungry feeling come o'er me stealing,
And the mice were squealing
in my prison cell
And that old triangle went jingle jangle,
Along the banks of the Royal Canal."

Brendan Behan
The Quare Fellow

Brendan Behan

1923-1964

"On the stage he was natural,
simple, affecting
'Twas only when he was off
he was acting."

Oliver Goldsmith
Retaliation

Oliver Goldsmith

1728-1792

On Pembroke Road look out for my ghost,
Dishevelled with shoes untied,
Playing through the railings with little children
Whose children have long since died.

Patrick Kavanagh
If you ever go to Dublin Town

Patrick Kavanagh

1904-1967

Brian O'Nolan wrote under the pseudonyms of Myles na gCopaleen and Flann O'Brien while he worked as a civil servant. He was perhaps the most satirical of all the Irish writers, Well remembered for his hugely funny column in the Irish Times.

Brian O'Nolan

1911-1966

"An' as it blowed an' blowed
I often looked up at the sky
an'assed meself the question,
what is the stars, what is the stars?"

Sean O'Casey
Juno and the Paycock

Sean O'Casey

1880-1964

"An Irishman's heart is nothing
but his imagination."

George Bernard Shaw
John Bull's other island

George Bernard Shaw

1856-1950

"Satire is a sort of glass wherin beholders
do generally discover
everybody's face but their own."

Jonathan Swift
Preface, Battle of the Books

Jonathan Swift

1667-1745

"A man who is not afraid of the sea
will soon be drowned, he said,
for he will be going out on a day he shouldn't.
But we do be afraid of the sea, and we do only
be drownded now and again."

John Millington Synge

John Millington Synge

1871-1909

"Do you really think it is weakness
that yields to temptation?
I tell you that there are terrible temptations
which it requires strength, strength and
courage to yield to.."

Oscar Wilde

Oscar Wilde

1854-1900

"We always find something, eh, Didi
to give us the impression that we exist."

Samuel Beckett
Waiting for Godot

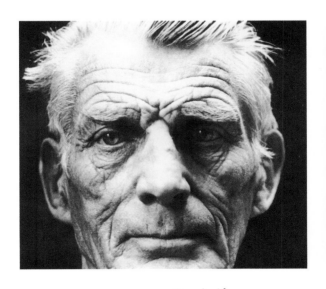

Samuel Beckett
1906-1989

"Come away, O human child!
To the waters and the wild
With a faery, hand in hand,
For the World's more full of weeping
than you can understand."

William Butler Yeats
The Stolen Child

William Butler Yeats

1865-1939

Although men are accused of not knowing
their own weakness, yet perhaps few know
their own strength.
It is in men as in soils, where sometimes
there is a vein of gold which the owner
knows not of.

Jonathan Swift

Permission for extracts courtesy of Faber & Faber for Beckett;
The Society of Authors for Shaw and Joyce; Methuen, London for
Behan; A.P. Watt for Yeats; Mac Millan Publishing for O'Casey and
Dr. Peter Kavanagh for Patrick Kavanagh.
Photographs courtesy of camera Press for Beckett, Shaw and
O'Casey; Yale University for Joyce; G.A. Duncan for Behan; The
Irish Times for Flann O'Brien; Hulton Picture Library for Yeats;
Film Illustration Library R.T.E. for Kavanagh; The Board of Trinity
College for Synge; The National Gallery For Swift and Goldsmith.